MW00755851

LIBERTY AND
EQUALITY

Liberty and Equality

RAYMOND ARON

Translated by Samuel Garrett Zeitlin
With a Preface by Mark Lilla and an
Epilogue by Pierre Manent

PRINCETON UNIVERSITY PRESS

PRINCETON & OXFORD

Original French edition established and presented by Pierre Manent of Raymond Aron's *Liberté et égalité*, © Éditions de l'EHESS, Paris, 2013

Published by Princeton University Press
41 William Street, Princeton, New Jersey 08540
99 Banbury Road, Oxford OX2 6JX

press.princeton.edu

All Rights Reserved

ISBN: 978-0-691-22676-7
ISBN: (e-book): 978-0-691-25091-5

British Library Cataloging-in-Publication Data is available

Editorial: Ben Tate and Josh Drake
Jacket design: Heather Hansen
Production: Danielle Amatucci
Publicity: Alyssa Sanford and Charlotte Coyne

This book has been composed in Arno

Printed on acid-free paper. ∞

Printed in the United States of America

10 9 8 7 6 5 4 3 2 1

A NOTE ON THE
TRANSLATION

The present book offers a translation of the edition established and presented by Pierre Manent of Raymond Aron's *Liberté et égalité, Cours au Collège de France* (Paris: Éditions de l'ÉHÉSS, 2013), with Pierre Manent's introduction to that volume translated and included here as an epilogue.

The present translation intends to offer a close and accurate translation of the French original within the limits of contemporary English, with the aim of conveying Aron's terminology, diction, political and philosophic vocabulary, whilst retaining the rhetorical figures and high diction within

Aron's lecture, not least by preserving Aron's word choice and syntax.

Aron's speech is not that of a Twitter user: his lecture is more Periclean than tweet-like, deploying the corresponding phrasings, elaborations, and high diction appropriate to a lecture at the heights of the French academic system, at the Collège de France.

TRANSLATOR'S
ACKNOWLEDGMENTS

With gratitude, I am thankful to Dominique
Schnapper, the Aron family, and Professor
Pierre Manent for the permission to publish
this translation. I am grateful to ÉHÉSS Édi-
tions and Princeton University Press, to
Anne Madelain, Daniel Mahoney, and Ben
Tate.

I am thankful to the Master of Corpus
Christi College in the University of Cam-
bridge, Professor Christopher Kelly, and to
Duncan Bell, Richard Bourke, Marina
Frasca-Spada, Shruti Kapila, Duncan Kelly,
JD Rhodes, Martin Ruehl, David Sneath, and
Harald Wydra for the chance to continue my

studies and teaching in Cambridge. No less, I am deeply thankful to Tim Byrnes, Noah Dauber, Robert Kraynak, Illan Nam, and Valerie Morkevičius for the privilege of teaching at Colgate University.

For helpful comments and assistance on earlier versions of this translation, I am thankful to Jenn Backer, Joshua Cherniss, Greg Conti, Daniel Cullen, Juan Fernando Ibarra Del Cueto, Hugo Drochon, Timothy Hampton, Olivier Hercend, Kinch Hoekstra, Victoria Kahn, Dominika Koter, Adam Lebovitz, Matt Luttig, Anne Madelain, Daniel Mahoney, Illan Nam, Or Rosenboim, Sam Rosenfeld, Blake Smith, Steven Smith, Daniel Steinmetz-Jenkins, Shannon Stimson, Becca Sugden, Ben Tate, and Joanna Williamson.

I am thankful for the love of my family—my mother, Elizabeth, my sister, Ellie, and my dear friend and companion, Joanna.

With gratitude and intellectual esteem, my work on this translation is dedicated to Professors Timothy Hampton and Shannon Stimson.

Samuel Garrett Zeitlin
Corpus Christi College,
University of Cambridge
July 2022

Mark Lilla

Russian bombs are falling on Ukraine this morning. Tanks are leveling homes, civilians are being shot. Miles-long queues of refugees are attempting to cross borders, any borders, before the battles reach them, while those able to fight remain to defend their homeland and their liberties. In Europe, old alliances are being revived and new lines are being drawn.

The Cold War as revenant.

It is a strangely propitious time, then, to reconsider Raymond Aron (1905–1983), the most prominent French liberal thinker of the Cold War period. Aron was born into a highly assimilated Jewish family and was set from an early age on the fixed French track toward high academic achievement. Yet in the early 1930s he made several trips to Germany, where he witnessed the rise of fascism and the inability of a democratic regime to confidently combat it. As Pierre Manent writes in the thoughtful essay included here, that experience made him the thinker we read and value today.

Aron came away from the 1930s with several fundamental insights. One was an appreciation of the value of the prosaic forms and rules of liberal democracy, which are there to prevent political life from descending into a raw struggle of all against all. Another was how fragile those forms can prove when confronted with passions nourished by myths of historical betrayal and future redemption—myths that became, as Aron later put it in the title of one of his books, the opium of the intellectuals. Having witnessed this, Aron conceived of a different model of intellectual life that would be less dramatic but more politically responsible, devoted to tolerance, reasonableness, scepticism, empiricism, and realism.

In post-war Paris, when the Marxism of Jean-Paul Sartre set the tone, there was no man more out of season than Raymond Aron. He and Sartre had once been friends and collaborated in founding *Les Temps Modernes* (Modern Times), the most influential intellectual journal of the period. Aron's collaboration soon ended, however, over disagreements about Communism and the Soviet Union. The deeper difference, though, was one of temperament. Sartre was entranced by the romantic myth of the political intellectual whose mode of engagement was the inspiring but uninformed pronouncement about the large forces shaping history, laced with contempt for those responsible for the machinery of government. Aron, by contrast, was interested in comprehending what he took to be the new social and international order forming in the wake of the two World Wars. He had more questions than answers, and wanted to understand this new world from within. As he wrote in his *Memoirs*, "For half a century I have restricted my own criticisms to posing this question—what would I do in their place?" Such questions were neither posed nor answered in *Les Temps Modernes*.

Shunned by Sartre and his epigones after the war, Aron found his audience in the French political and academic establishment, teaching at the Collège de France and writing an influential column in the conservative paper *Le Figaro*. Yet he insisted on calling himself a liberal, not a conservative, and he was right to.

The French liberal tradition is very different from the British and American ones. In the anglosphere, discourse about liberty and liberalism tends to be moral and formalistic; what matters is enumerating individual human rights and then inscribing them in law. The French tradition, beginning with 19th century figures like Benjamin Constant and Alexis de Tocqueville, has always been more sociological and psychological in approach. Democracy is regarded as a historically specific type of society with a characteristic way of life, within which certain rational principles like individual rights have currency; yet those principles are complemented by, and to some extent undergirded by, non-rational norms, codes, habits, rituals, beliefs, and feelings. Understanding liberal democracy, in this view, requires paying attention to these two levels of political life and how they interact.

This is the approach Raymond Aron takes in this lecture on liberty, the last he gave as member of the Collège de France, in 1978. It is not an inspirational text. It is instead a characteristically clarifying one that distinguishes between different forms of liberty and reflects on the human characteristics required—virtues—to maintain it. The lecture also offers some lessons for today. For example, besides considering the concept of freedom, Aron also asks what it is that makes us *feel* free—which, in terms of human action, is the crucial question. No matter how much liberty the laws may give us, he reminds us, if we feel that the political and economic order are fundamentally illegitimate we will feel unfree. And no amount of lawyerly arguing or philosophical reasoning will dislodge that feeling. Something else must be done. An important insight at a time when liberal democracies just about everywhere are under populist challenge.

At the very end of his life Aron was rediscovered by a new generation of French intellectuals who identified with the left but had broken free of Marxism after the revelations of Alexander Solzhenitsyn's *The Gulag Archipelago* (translated in 1973) and the Cambodian genocide. A new appreciation of liberal democratic life was developing, and along with it an appreciation of Aron's writing. In a remarkable turn of the table, a group of these young thinkers in 1979 invited Raymond Aron and Jean-Paul Sartre both to a meeting with French president Valéry Giscard d'Estaing to demand assistance for the refugees fleeing Communist Vietnam and Cambodia. It was clear to all involved who had been vindicated.

Sometimes it takes a direct confrontation with despotism to remind us of the value of the liberties we enjoy. May that happen again when the guns finally fall silent in Ukraine.

New York City, April 2022

LIBERTY AND
EQUALITY

Note to the Reader

The text which one is about to read is that of the last lecture of Raymond Aron at the Collège de France, delivered on April 4, 1978. The recording having been lost, it has been edited from a very faulty handwritten transcript by Giulio De Ligio and Pierre Manent, who have had to make choices "according to the spirit." Such as it is, it gives a faithful idea of the political perspective of Raymond Aron at the twilight of his university career.

I would like to consecrate this last lecture, as I had informed you, to liberty, or more precisely *to liberties*. I don't like employing the word liberty in the singular. Just as one sometimes says that peace is indivisible—which is not true—, one sometimes says that liberty is indivisible, which is equally false. Even in the most despotic societies, individuals enjoy certain liberties. In order to understand this, it suffices to employ liberty in the most prosaic sense, and one sees that the individual who has the possibility of choosing between this and that, of doing or not doing, of going to the church or of not going there, is at liberty with respect to this particular activity, and that in this sense, there are *liberties*. We all enjoy certain liberties, and we never enjoy all of the liberties. In practice, in order that we may enjoy certain liberties, it is necessary to prohibit other fellow citizens from preventing us (one must stop them from stopping us) exercising our liberties. When we want to organize a public demonstration, in order for it to take place it is necessary to exclude others, or prevent them from preventing our demonstration. This means: there is no liberty for something or for someone which does not, most of the time, reciprocally bear a restriction or prohibition for something else or for someone else.

Of course, if we reason in the manner of the philosophers of the 17th or of the 18th century, if we refer ourselves to the state of nature, the problem poses itself differently.

One may say that, in the state of nature when there has not been a state of society, liberty is confounded with the capacity or with the power of the individual. Certain philosophers have analyzed the state of nature as that in which the liberty of each is confounded with his power. The individual has to battle with nature, he is free to do whatever his force gives him the capacity to do, but there are also the others, and since he has not yet tied social bonds with the others he may find himself with them in a situation of peace, or he may find himself in a situation of war.

As you know, certain philosophers have characterized the state of nature as the war of all against all. The striking example is that of Hobbes, who had elsewhere compared the state of nature which he describes with the relation of States to one another. The States, according to him, in effect, are in the state of nature, that is to say in a permanent state of war, be it real or simply potential. Others on the contrary, like Montesquieu, have not described the state of nature as a state of war where each wants to get the upper hand over the other, but as a state in which humans would be fearful, frightened, and as a result would never have the idea of domination or the instinct of violence. I am not sure that one can settle the debate between these different interpretations of the state of nature because these interpretations reflect different theories of human nature. And even better, it seems to me, not to refer to the situation of humans in the Paleolithic age, which we know poorly, but rather to refer at the same time to what we know in the small Neolithic societies and in our societies.

All that one may affirm as certain or almost certain is that beyond society insecurity reigns amongst humans. I think that almost all the philosophers who utilized this notion of the state of nature recognized that, without a power superior to all the individuals, without a power capable of imposing peace, there is, at the very least, a situation of insecurity. It is thus quite significant that Montesquieu, in *The Spirit of the Laws*, defines political liberty in the following terms: "Political liberty consists in surety, or at least in the opinion one has of one's surety" (Book XII, chapter 2). And surety comes in third place in the enumeration of fundamental rights in article 2 of the *Declaration of the Rights of Man and Citizen* of 1789. One may furthermore join to the term surety that of property, which the same article places in the second rank of the enumeration, right after liberty. There is not surety for a human individual if he is not protected in what he has, in what is proper to him. Not that I want to imply or insinuate that any property may play the role of surety. All societies promulgate laws which govern property, which determine what form of property is legitimate and what form of property is not legitimate. What seems incontestable is that in every society, even in a totally socialist society, there is something which is the property of the individual, of such a sort that one may say that surety and property make up part of the fundamental rights—the content of property being, once again, determined by the laws of the society considered.

It results from all this that to posit or to deduce liberty in the abstract does not mean very much. One of my auditors has reminded me of a famous definition of liberty: "Liberty consists in the power to do whatever does not harm another; thus the exercise of the natural rights of each man is only limited by those which assure to other members of the same society the enjoyment of the same rights. These limits may only be determined by the law." Without doubt you have recognized article 4 of the same *Declaration* of 1789. Who would not accept this formula, at least to the extent to which one does not seek to define exactly the sense of the words? In effect, it follows, so to speak, self-evidently, that each person may be free in the whole extent to which he does not harm others. But, to take a particularly significant example in modern society, how is one to verify that the economic activity of one does not harm others?

In other words, this formula is, at once, in one sense evident and in another sense almost denuded of meaning. Let us suppose, to take another example, that in deploying your liberty of thought you should critique in an extreme manner the policy of the government, that you should condemn the law or war which the government declares or wages: in an evident manner, you do harm to certain persons, to those who apply or who sustain the law or the policy of the government. As a consequence, in fact, it seems to me always difficult to define in a precise or meaningful manner the content of liberty or of the liberties. Among societies certain liberties are considered as legitimate and necessary and others are unknown. Certain liberties which we enjoy and which, for us, are fundamental, have been considered as indifferent or were unknown in other societies. Therefore, without pretending to make a general theory of liberties for all societies, I will attempt here and now to specify what is the content of our liberties, in our democratic, prosperous, and liberal countries—which are all these things or would like to be.

The Liberties in the Liberal Democracies

These liberties are those which the public power recognizes to individuals and guarantees to them. As a consequence, these are the liberties which, in order that we may enjoy them, ought to be guaranteed by the prohibitions addressed to those who would stop us from exercising them. I shall distinguish four categories of liberties.

The first is the surety or the protection of the individuals. The paradox, in any case the difficulty of this first category of liberties, is that they are at once guaranteed by the police and by the judiciary and also guaranteed against the abuses of the judiciary or of the police. One of the essential components of the liberties in the eyes of the men of the 18th century was the protection against the abuse of the judiciary, whose vocation it nevertheless was to protect the individuals. In the same way, today, the law grants guarantees against the police, but on the other hand, the passion for security, or the desire for surety, which is extremely strong in our societies, makes us demand more from the police—this same police which we curse in a general manner and which we call for in our prayers in certain circumstances. Perhaps there are countries where the ambivalence of this sentiment is attenuated. Amongst ourselves this ambivalence is strong and the same persons show very different sentiments with regard to the police according to the circumstances. A second category of liberties is summed up by the liberty of free movement—in the interior of our country and across the borders of our country. We are free to move ourselves across the whole territory without asking the permission of anyone. We also have the right, if we are in revolt against the policy of our country, to choose another country and, after several years, to become a citizen there. A liberty which, elsewhere, has been relatively rare in history. A third category concerns the choice of employment or the choice of work. This pertains to the economic liberties which include the free choice of the consumer and the freedom of enterprise of the entrepreneurs. The fourth category comprehends religious liberty and, in a general manner, the liberty of opinion, of expression, of communication.

To be sure, all the liberties of this first series are imperfect. One could write books to show that the judiciary system is extremely manipulated by the public power. One could write black books on the police, etc. But, compared with what happens in other countries, we may say that in the majority of countries that I am considering, which is to say those of Western Europe, these liberties are tolerably guaranteed or assured. In the fourth category I have placed together religion and opinions in general, because in secularized societies political convictions become or tend to become the equivalent of what religious convictions were in the past. In any case, the group of liberties which I come to enumerate, I call the *personal liberties*. And apart from religion, from the opinions or the convictions, I arrive at a second group which I shall call the *political liberties*.

The *political liberties* may be summed up by three words: voting, protesting, and assembling. And here again, we may say that we tolerably enjoy these political liberties.

The third category, these are the *social liberties*, which one often calls the social rights, but I think that one may equally well call them the social liberties. I shall say that the social liberties are those which the majority, or even, if possible, the totality of the population enjoys, due to its own means or due to the specific means which the State furnishes to those who are in need: the first idea for social security was that of giving to all the material means of exercising certain liberties, like the liberty of being cared for, or that of being educated. Within these social liberties there is a subcategory: the liberty of collectives. This concerns union strike actions, the services rendered by the work councils, the objective of which is, in addition to improving the conditions of the salaried workers, to attenuate the omnipotence of the bosses of the firms and to introduce in the life of the firm something which would be more conformable to the aspirations of the democracy. As I have said to you many times, one of the fundamental contradictions of our societies is that professional life is not organized according to democratic principles. From there, the liberties of the collectives, of the unions or of the work councils would attenuate, or soften, the authoritarian hierarchy which exists in the large firms. The liberty of the unions, that is to say, the liberty of the individuals who assemble themselves in the unions, leads naturally to a rivalry of power between the bosses and those who represent the workers.

This distinction between three categories, personal liberties, political liberties, social liberties, does not recapitulate in any way the distinction which has today become current between formal liberties and material or real liberties. Indeed, personal liberties which I mentioned at the beginning are, evidently, real liberties *par excellence*. Nothing is more real than being able to move to another city, leave one's own country, or sometimes choose one's country. It is not a concern, in the case of the personal liberties, of something formal which does not touch what is essential; exactly the contrary, I would say that these personal liberties are essentially or eminently concrete. And if ordinarily it is difficult to think about it, it's because these personal liberties have become at a certain point part of our normal and evident manner of life to such an extent that it would be necessary for these liberties to be violated or eliminated in order for us to be cognizant of their eminent value.

The social liberties which I mentioned in the third instance are equally and to the same degree real liberties. They are in effect the necessary conditions of the exercise of certain liberties, or even it's an attempt to attenuate the power gap between those who hold authority and those who submit to authority. For as long as there are those in our societies who command and those in our societies who obey, the organization of those who obey for the purpose of attenuating the abuses will be a necessity justified by the principles which we invoke.

In what concerns the second category, the political liberties, it is more difficult to give the answer: is it a matter of formal liberties or of real liberties? I would say that, in fact, political liberties such as I have defined them have simultaneously an eminent symbolic value and indirectly a considerable efficacity in most circumstances. Why do the political liberties such as those defined by the right to vote have an extraordinary symbolic value? Because the right to vote consecrates, so to speak, the equality of all individuals, despite all the inequalities, in relation to something which is essential in itself, which is to say the choice of those who govern. Of course, one can say that it's essentially a symbol—and it's true—, but experience tells us that electoral procedures, or representative procedures, are in the end an effective form of liberty, in the sense that in the interior of a society where electoral procedures are respected in their spirit, much of the violence and the injustice afflicting the societies which ignore these procedures are foreseen and corrected. One can say that the infinitesimal power of each person on election day is but a symbol, and it's true: we never choose directly, except in the presidential election, those who govern us, and when we choose them directly, our voice is but one among millions. One can also say, which is still true as well, that it's always a set menu, because it constrains us to choose between two people, and perhaps we would have preferred a third person. One can say that this corners us, in the legislative elections, into choosing between two blocks while we ourselves, we would prefer to be "elsewhere." In this sense it is perfectly true that the electoral act or the parliamentary procedure does not necessarily grant people the feeling that they govern themselves. It is perfectly true that, to begin with, representative government has a symbolic value, but it is also true that, in a manner not secondary but primary, the existence of the procedures, the necessity for those who govern of presenting themselves anew before those who have elected them, does not constitute an absolute guarantee against the abuses of power or against despotism, but all the same a form of protection and, so to speak, a rampart. Briefly, above all if one takes account of our experiences of the 20th century, one may consider these political liberties, which I have inserted between personal liberties and social liberties, as perhaps the most symbolically significant form of liberty and at the same time, in a measure variable according to the case, as the essential condition of the other liberties.

One may also present the liberties in our societies in the following manner: our liberties are defined at once thanks to the State and against it. Throughout the centuries the liberties of individuals have been conceived as resistances to the abuses of the State, of limits on its omnipotence, but simultaneously, in the societies in which we live, we expect the guarantee of certain of our liberties from the State. It's particularly striking in the case of surety, which is defined as owing to the State and often against it. With respect to the liberty of critique, which the intellectual inevitably considers as an essential liberty, it presupposes that one may express oneself against the State, which ought, therefore, for its part, to guarantee the possibility of doing so. The condition is that the State be of a democratic type, which is to say that it ought not to be a partisan State and that it confounds itself with neither a religion nor an ideology. Perhaps it's dangerous for a State to only define itself negatively, by the rejection of an ideology, or by the liberty given to all ideologies, but the fact is that our regimes define themselves in this way. In what concerns the social liberties, these too derive from the protection or from the assistance of the State, or of the unions, assistance and protection which augments the individual power of the workers. With respect to the third kind of liberties, the liberties of the citizen, their heart is evidently the liberty of participation in the State through the intermediary of procedures, electoral and other, which we know.

Consciousness of Liberty and Representation of the Good Society

I have left aside, in an intentional way, two questions on which one may speak for a long time. I have left aside completely the question of the *feeling* of liberty but I am quite ready to recognize that in a society with the principles I am describing, many individuals have the feeling of not being free. To begin with, all those who detest the existing regime judge themselves to be oppressed. First, they are perhaps oppressed because there is always oppression to a lesser or greater degree in an unequal society like our own; but, in any case, it suffices that the members of society consider the system of authority, such as it is, to be unjust in order for them not to experience the feeling of liberty. In other words, the conditions or circumstances which grant the feeling of liberty are multiple and variable; they are in large measure impossible to determine in a systematic manner even though one can possibly, as I have tried to do, specify the content of the different liberties. For the moment, let us accept this: our society, which the majority of us consider a society of liberties, may be resented by a part of the population as a society of oppression, by reason of the material circumstances in which these persons live, and also for another reason which may be treated later, to wit, their representation of the good society. In as much as they consider that contemporary society, specifically because it involves individual proprietary ownership of the means of production, is in itself unjust, these members of society feel themselves deprived of liberty because they do not recognize the legitimacy of the system of power, nor of the economic and social order in its entirety. I would willingly say that the consciousness of liberty does not separate itself from the consciousness of the legitimacy of the society, and this depends in large part on the sentiments which stem from the degree of inequality and the system of authority. It is therefore difficult to know if, and in what circumstances, humans experience the feeling of being free in a certain society, because the ideology of each person is at least one of the principal causes of the feeling of liberty, or, on the contrary, of the feeling of the absence of liberty.

Aside from this, we also know that the professional discipline which exists in the firms is resented by a part of the population of workers as a system of unfreedom, and that this impression of unfreedom can only be attenuated by a less hierarchic organization of labor or even by an increased adherence by the laborers to the system itself. American workers in their immense majority adhere to the system of the individual proprietary ownership of capital; as a result they feel themselves less oppressed by an organization of labor, which is in their own eyes legitimate or acceptable, than those who live in a society where an important part of the population explicitly refuses to accept the legitimacy of the system and by consequence the authority of those who command.

Finally, I have left aside entirely, and voluntarily, another problem which would require at least another lecture: that of the liberty of the collectivity itself. Because it is self-evident that when a group, which is distinguished by certain characteristics, claims autonomy or independence in relation to the political body in which it is integrated, this is because this group feels oppressed. The liberty which is thereby sought is collective liberty, the liberty of the group in its entirety. This is not what I have sought to analyze here, which is to say, the liberty of the individuals within a political community. After all, in Greek antiquity, the liberty of the cities was primordial. Liberty *par excellence* was the liberty of the group, of the city. And even today, effectively, there is a problem which I have left aside, that of the liberty of the collectives or of the groups— national or otherwise.

My enumeration of the liberties obviously possesses an empirical and historical character. It is self-evident that some of these liberties would not have meaning in societies other than our own. For example, it is difficult to imagine for the small Neolithic societies the right of choosing one's tribe as a fundamental right. The prohibition made against Soviet citizens changing countries appears scandalous to us, but there are innumerable societies across history in which a prohibition of this order would not even have made sense: the very possibility of leaving one's country or of choosing one's country, of choosing the conditions in which one intends to live, supposes in large measure a civilization like our own, which protects and even encourages the free activity of each person. In the same way, in the societies where the monarchic principle was recognized as legitimate by the whole population, the idea of choosing those who are to govern by the intermediary of an election, or the idea of representative government, could not occur to the members of this collectivity, essentially different from our own. All this, of course, does not prohibit seeking and even finding certain rights of man with a universal value, but these universal rights have therefore an abstract character which may neither enlighten us nor guide us, so that it does not appear to me essential to search in this direction. What I wish to suggest by means of this summary is that the liberties which I have mentioned one after another cover the essence of what we understand in Europe, including perhaps in Eastern Europe, to be our essential liberties.

Philosophic Stakes and Experiences of Liberty

From here two problems pose themselves, which I am obliged to treat very rapidly despite their complexity. First off, what are the stakes concerning these liberties which are truly decisive, truly essential? What are those stakes which the different parties consider as deserving primacy? Which of these liberties may be considered as liberty *par excellence*? And the second problem is the following: what is the relation between the political and social liberties such as I have analyzed them, and the philosophy of liberty? And primarily, is there some relation between the politics of liberty and the philosophy of liberty?

First problem: the stakes, that which is essential in this ensemble of liberties. Which out of these liberties may be considered as liberty *par excellence*? I said to you that I prefer not to speak of *liberty*, because one can only define liberty *par excellence* in two ways: either by elaborating a vision of the good society, which is to say establishing a hierarchy among the various liberties and choosing those which in our eyes define the good society such as it ought to be, or, more summarily, by choosing the liberties which in our eyes are essential from the perspective of a political ideology.

For a long time in the West, let us say since the development of socialism, discussion has been conducted on the relative importance of what I have called the social liberties, which is to say liberties in civil society, and the political liberties which are defined in relation to the State, and more precisely to the participation of citizens in political life. From this fact there has been, across the whole of the 19th century, and the 20th century above all, a debate between those who uphold the primacy of political liberties—the democrats—and those who uphold the social liberties—the socialists. The debate continues but, it seems to me, with less passion, at least in

France and Western Europe, because experience, or history if you wish, has proffered its lesson, and a severe lesson at that. In Marxism, or in a certain interpretation of Marxism, one finds a major idea, which is that whatever the political regime may be, whether it be despotic or representative, individual ownership of the means of production implies a dictatorship of the bourgeoisie. This is an idea you find everywhere. It was the renewed object of discussion when the French Communist Party rejected the doctrine of the dictatorship of the proletariat. Indeed, one finds this idea in a great number of texts by Lenin, in some rather rare texts of Marx and in a great number of texts of the Althusserians, for example, today. One may summarily describe these matters in the following way: from the moment when one supposes that in civil society, or in economic activity, there is necessarily a dominant class, and in addition when one calls this class domination a dictatorship, one may say that as long as this social structure is not modified, there is a dictatorship of the bourgeoisie. Therefore, in order to pass from the capitalist regime to the socialist regime, it is necessary that another class substitute itself for the bourgeoisie in order to exercise this hegemony or this dictatorship. Assuredly, if one abandons the notion of the dictatorship of the proletariat, if one thereby renounces the necessity of a phase of the dictatorship of the proletariat, indirectly one abandons the original idea of Marxism, or of a certain interpretation of Marxism, to wit, that whatever the political regime may be, the society is submitted to the dictatorship or domination of one class.

According to Soviet ideology today, after having suppressed individual proprietary ownership of the means of production, and at the same time having eliminated the dictatorship of the bourgeoisie in order to substitute the dictatorship of the proletariat in its place, the Soviets have constructed a society in which the dictatorship of the proletariat has become unnecessary, in which there is no longer a dominant class, a classless society. What removes a major part of the force of this argument is that the simple observation of communist societies suffices to demonstrate two very simple facts: on the one hand, that state power since the revolution has been exercised by a minority, by the party, and that it has never been exercised by the proletariat; and, on the other hand, that this dominant minority in the State also exercises the ruling powers in civil society, which, in large measure, is confounded with the State itself. Hence, what happens is a reduction, violation, or elimination of the personal liberties which were essential to the so-called bourgeois democracy, an integral part of the bourgeois heritage. Indeed, this bourgeois heritage, Marx or Engels never wanted to eliminate it; they never thought that the elimination of the dictatorship of the bourgeoisie would simultaneously entail the elimination of the personal liberties. Experience appears therefore to indicate that the very principle of this theory is false: there always exist, at least in the societies such as we know them in modern civilization, ruling minorities. We are disposed to admit that in the civil society of democracies, whether it be in industry or in banks, there is a minority who exert a decisive influence and, in this sense, exercise the domination of man over man. But one is obliged to add according to a jest known in the Soviet world: "What's the difference between socialism and capitalism?

In the one case, it's the exploitation of man by man, in the other, it's the reverse." Or still, let us say, the domination of man by man exists in all societies known at the present time; what differentiates between societies is the mode of exercising this power by the ruling minorities and the guarantees that the State or these powers are able to give to the governed.

One consequence of all this is that today liberalism tends to define itself, in a manner perhaps regrettable, essentially by its opposition to totalitarianism. In the past, liberalism was founded on philosophic doctrines. Today, I am inclined to believe that liberalism (because this doctrine is ascribed to me) justifies itself in a negative or defensive, sometimes aggressive manner, as an alternative to totalitarianism, an alternative validated by historical experience. In fact, in the totalitarian regimes of the 20th century liberalism rediscovered all the enemies which it had combatted in the course of its history. Indeed, liberalism defined itself first of all against the absolutism of a religion, and we find ourselves confronted with the absolutism of an ideology. We defend the right of each person to seek *her* truth, and in this sense, the claim against the absolutism of an ideology situates itself in the wake of the liberal or Enlightenment claim against religious absolutism. What we claim today is the distinction between the State which we indirectly choose by our votes, and the truth of society or of the good society. The liberal regime even accepts that the liberal principle itself may be questioned and, in this sense, we come upon an extreme form of the original liberalism. In the same way, because Montesquieu considered liberty as beginning with surety, it seems to me that the totalitarian experience has restored the value of this security. The societies in which we live do not all guarantee the liberty that is desirable, but they avoid the extreme forms of the privation of liberty which we have known across this century.

Finally, one of the grand ideas of the liberal democratic movement was to progressively introduce the constitutional principle into the government of men, and today the democratic procedures, organized by a Constitution, assure, on the one hand, the participation of individuals in the government and, on the other hand, limit the arbitrary power of the governors by the laws. Whatever one may think of the conduct of President Nixon and of the Watergate episode, the fact is that the possibility, in a Constitution, of removing the president of the Republic[1] by the intermediary

---

1. Aron's French text uses the vocabulary for describing the French president in the Fifth Republic ("le président

of the power of the judiciary, conforms to one of the original aspirations of liberal thought. The resignation of President Nixon represents the extreme consequence of a Constitution which has no equivalent elsewhere, in which the power of the judiciary is above the executive power as well as the legislative power, and which thus consecrates legal procedure in the exercise of power. The guarantee of legality in the exercise of power is something extraordinarily rare in history. I am well aware that this legality is not always maintained, even in our regimes, but the ideal subsists and some examples prove that the ideal is sometimes effective.

That said, the last thing I want is to leave the impression that we are coming to a

de la République") to describe the office of the US president.—Trans.

consensus. The debate continues. It bears in particular on the inequalities which relate to resources or opportunities. The more we are drawn to defining liberty by the capacity or the power of doing, the more inequality appears to us unacceptable. Likewise, insofar as one tends to confound liberty and equality more and more, every form of inequality appears a violation of liberty. If you want to see the pure expression of what I believe to be an error or an illusion, read the book recently published under the direction of Robert Badinter, *Liberty, liberties* [*Liberté, libertés*].[2] There one finds total confusion between liberty and equality. The authors observe

2. [Note of the editors to the French original:] *Liberté, libertés. Réflexions du comité pour une charte des libertés animé par Robert Badinter*, préface de François Mitterrand, Paris, Gallimard, 1976.

that those who have more resources, more means, those who are higher in the social hierarchy, are more free than others. If one defines liberty by power, this proposition is evident. But if one retains the strict and rigorous sense of liberty—liberty as equal right—, then equality of rights may not find expression, in an inegalitarian society, in the equality of powers. One can give all persons access to the universities; one cannot make it that all access the same universities, in any case not to the same success at university. I leave aside the pessimistic books which see a degradation of the situation of individual rights in our societies, like *Abandoned liberties* [*Les libertés à l'abandon*] by Roger Errera,[3] where a considerable number of violations or things

---

3. [Note of the editors to the French original:] Roger Errera, *Les libertés à l'abandon*, Paris, Seuil, 1978.

missing from our principles or from our
ideas are mentioned.

The Total Rejection of Society as a
New Mode of Thought

This being said, something new is produc-
ing itself in the way of thinking in continen-
tal Europe which makes us depart from the
discussion in which I have been occupied
today, which is to say a discussion which
has up until the present remained within an
essentially traditional frame. Indeed, one of
the ideological tendencies which, it seems
to me, at the present hour has the greatest
success with the younger generation, is the
detestation of power as such. We here arrive at another phase of the discussion, or
at a wholly other discussion. Those who are
called the New Philosophers, the generation
which today denounces the Soviet regime

and the gulag, have not ended up accepting liberal societies, at least not up until now. What they refuse in the end is power itself; what they discover or believe themselves to discover, and surely this exists, is the network of power, or power as network. If one defines power by the action or influence of one upon another, we are in a network, in innumerable networks of power: the student is in a network of power in his relation to the professor; the workers are in the network of power of the firm; the bosses of the firm are in a network of power in relation to the management, etc. Society being inegalitarian and bearing within it a certain number of collective activities, where there is society there is evidently power. But to eliminate power in professional life means either that one can do without bosses (which seems unlikely, whatever one's hopes in worker self-management), or that the central power has withered away, and in this case what one really wants is decentralization or the multiplication of groups or command centers. Finally, one can place one's hopes in an idea, a representation which seems to me to inspire this generation: something which sometimes is defined as community, sometimes as anarchy.

I fear that these two notions may be rather antipodal to one another, but one finds as an obsession, for example in the book of Robert Badinter, the idea of community, which is to say the idea that individuals find true liberty in community. Surely, it is possible that the individual finds liberty in a fraternal community, and not in competition or in solitude. But it is also possible that the narrow community may become despotic very rapidly. I am not sure that the community of the village was anarchic as such, or that it guaranteed liberty for individuals. In the same way, I am not sure that the power of the unions would always be a guarantee for the liberty of the workers who do not belong to unions, or who would prefer not to belong to unions. But we ought to observe that there is today a movement in this direction, and that liberalism such as we define it, which is to say a pluralism of liberties and powers, this liberalism which accompanies an authoritarian system in professional or economic life, is considered by many as the very essence of oppression. Failing to find a representation of the good society in Marxism or Sovietism, there is no longer a search for the good society but a total rejection of the existing society. This radical rejection sometimes takes a pacifist form (the communes, the "hippies"[4]), and sometimes takes a violent form, as you well know.

4. The term "hippies" is English in the French original.—Trans.

Political Liberty and
Philosophic Liberty

I arrive now at the last point, to wit, the relation between political liberty and philosophic liberty. Up to the present moment, I have defined, during this lecture, liberty simply as intentional action, action which consists in choice and which presupposes for the individual the possibility of doing or of not doing. Indeed, without doubt, the philosophers give a richer and more precise sense to liberty. Montesquieu, for his part, says that the liberty of the philosopher was the exercise of will. I am not sure that this would be the definition which all the philosophers would have given, but let us say that there is a great philosophic tradition according to which authentic liberty is the mastery of reason or of the will over the passions. Liberty *par excellence* would be reflective thought, the thought process guided by a reason dominating the passions. From here, certain philosophies of liberty may more or less confound the politics of liberty and the philosophy of liberty. Indeed, philosophy and politics coincide when both assume the reasonable man by hypothesis. They do not necessarily assume the good man; they presuppose him perhaps, or probably, to be egoistic and calculating, with desires, perhaps even with passions. But the politics of liberty more often assumed the reasonable man not as a postulate or as a condition but as an objective, and supposed that if free society had an objective, it was to create free men, and that men would only be really, authentically free to the extent to which they obey not any caprice whatsoever, not any passion whatsoever, but reason, the reason which makes them accept citizenship, which is to say the reason which makes them accept the laws of society.

The man in society who obeys the laws is in a certain manner already a free man, in the political sense and even in the philosophic sense: he obeys himself, at least in a democratic regime, and he accomplishes what is best for himself. He realizes himself as a free man in obeying the law. And if there is not a coincidence between civic spirit and morality, one may at least say that civic spirit is a part of morality. Now, this representation of the free society as permitting the formation of free men, I am not sure that it would still be the dominant philosophy among us. Kant, in order to represent a good society, imagined free and responsible men, guided by the commandments of reason. Now, I believe that today, in the majority of Western societies, liberty essentially means the liberation of the desires. Not only are we in a hedonistic society, that's obvious, but I would say also that today, the enemy is the State or power qua the enemy of individual desires; the enemy is also all the prohibitions and all the institutions which, in effect, limit the liberty of the individual as a being of desire.

Perhaps I err in taking too seriously and in considering as central a certain philosophy which is in fashion in Paris today. Yet I think that in fact, in the assemblage of Western societies, when one invokes the idea of the free society, the idea of liberty, it's not in order to invite individuals to obey the laws or to govern themselves according to the rational law, but rather in order to incite them to express their personality such as it is and to follow their desires such as they are. Assuredly, John Stuart Mill

himself, in the book *On Liberty*[5] on which
I offered a commentary for you several
weeks ago, also said that society ought to
offer a total liberty to individuals to the
extent that their way of life, even if it was
shocking, did not harm others. And in this
sense, Mill conceived liberty essentially
as the possibility, the legitimacy for the individual of living after his fashion, debauched
if he wanted to be, miserly if he so wished,
odious with those near to him if this was his
disposition; such conduct called for moral
censure, but not for any intervention whatsoever by the public powers. Today, liberty
is defined in our societies by repressing the
reality principle and by the liberation of the

---

5. [Note of the editors of the French edition:] John
Stuart Mill, *On Liberty*, New York, H. Holt and Company,
1905. [The title of *On Liberty* is given in English in the
French original.—Trans.]

pleasure principle, the liberation of *eros*. Whence, it seems to me, derives what one calls the moral crisis of liberal democracies. Indeed, every regime must define itself first by a notion of legitimacy, and then by an ideal. With respect to legitimacy, I think that our democracies have more or less succeeded. I think that, in particular thanks to the comparison with the Soviet experience, the electoral procedures and the personal liberties are considered as something essential by Westerners, including the immense majority of the French, whatever, moreover, their other political options may be. But what one no longer knows today in our democracies is where virtue is to be found. Because the theories of democracy and the theories of liberalism always included something like the definition of the virtuous citizen or the manner of life which would conform to the ideal of a free society.

Our societies are legitimate in the eyes of the members, but they have no other ideal than that of permitting to each the choice of one's path. I share this ideal. I participate in this manner of thinking of the society in which I live. But as an observer of societies in history, I ask myself: is it possible to give stability to democratic regimes of which the principle of legitimacy is election and of which the ideal is the right or the liberty for everyone of choosing not only one's path in life, which is just, but in addition one's conception of good and evil? The fact is that today it seems to me extremely difficult whether in the high schools or in the universities to speak seriously of the duties of the citizens. I think that whoever risks doing this would seem like one who belongs to a world which has disappeared.

It's an idea which Malraux expressed in diverse forms more than once. Like him,

I am no longer sure whether in our societies there is still a representation of the good society, nor a representation of the ideal or accomplished man. Perhaps this species of scepticism which underlies liberalism is the necessary result of the development of our civilizations. One may not stop posing questions, all the more so given that in the face of our societies there are others which have a different principle of legitimacy and which attempt to teach both their principle of legitimacy and their representation of the good society and of the virtuous man. More-over, I am not sure that this indoctrination such as one may encounter it elsewhere has really succeeded. I simply state this and content myself with fixing the point at which we find ourselves.

I have not taken new research into con-sideration. Today, one does research, on the one hand, in animal ethology, and, on the

other hand, in the biology of human societies. One better understands the social
mechanism. All this is found beyond the
traditional discussions in which I have remained. I have remained there, not because
I am ignorant of later research, but because
the research in biology, or in ethology,
is not conclusive and they leave us for
the moment in the situation which I have
attempted to describe.

The Happy Exception of
Free Societies

A last word, which is not a conclusion but
a marginal remark. At root, all that I have
said only deeply concerns a small part of
humanity. My reflections on the relations
between liberty and equality, on the claims
of equality in liberty, concern the phenom-

ena of Western societies, that is to say, of relatively prosperous societies and those which have a deep tradition of seeking liberty in equality or equality in liberty. Now, if we imagine that our societies only represent a feeble part of humanity, it is necessary to say that these problems, which are still ours, these debates which still have, I believe, a meaning, these philosophic speculations which still make nourishment for our thoughts, all this is, all the same, specifically, and perhaps narrowly, Western. I do not want at all to say that the populations of Africa or of Asia are indifferent to the problem of equality such as I have posed it or to the problem of liberty such as I have discussed it. I do not believe that whatever we do or think, we others in the West, ought to be provincial. But these are the problems and thoughts of privileged societies—of privileged societies which have, so to speak, determined the vocabulary and the discourses of other peoples, of other societies, in placing at the center of attention questions which are probably not, for many other peoples, the most urgent questions.

I don't want to conclude anything. I am simply saying that our societies, the imperfections of which we critique with a just title, represent today, in relation to the majority of the societies of the world, a happy exception. The societies which we describe and which we critique, these societies which live by permanent debate concerning the order which ought to be, these societies which make power move toward rule-bound and pacific conflict between the groups and the parties, are historically exceptional societies. I do not conclude that they are condemned to die. Still less do I conclude that the societies of the rest of humanity are called to organize their communal life on our model. I say that we ought never to forget, to the extent that we love liberties or liberty, that we enjoy a privilege rare in history and rare in space.

Epilogue

POLITICS AS SCIENCE AND AS CONCERN

Pierre Manent

The work of Raymond Aron is like politics itself: apparently easy of access and nonetheless difficult to know in its last resort and in its ultimate ends.

We approach politics with our passions, which we believe to be generous, and our opinions, which we believe to be enlightened. It is thus that citizens of modern democracies spontaneously proceed, and

Aron himself began or begins thus. Having arrived at old age, he gave his *Memoirs* the following subtitle: *50 years of political reflection*. In truth, this meant to say: fifty years of political *education*.[1] This is because one is never a perfectly enlightened citizen. One is never entirely in the clear with one's passions and one's opinions. To understand politics is therefore an education, an exercise in humanity which is never completed, because the experience of the actions and of the speeches of men always retains its surprises, and the experience poses questions which we did not ourselves await. Aron scrutinized political life with tireless attention up until his last day, because he was unable to retire from the place where humanity challenges itself.

1. Italics present in the French original.—Trans.

Aron has evoked his formative years
with sufficient precision.[2] He reached the
age of maturity, as one calls it, at the epoch
in which European politics had begun to
endanger European civilization. Indeed, it
was about to bring it to the brink of annihi-
lation. The first education which Aron received still expressed confidence in progress—the progress of society and of culture
which appeared to be an ascertainable fact
as well as an acquired right. Even after the
Great War, the reigning intellectual disci-
plines, each in its own language, betrayed
this confidence in the movement of society
and of the human spirit. Aron had to make

2. [Note to the French original:] Beyond his *Mémoires*
(Paris, Julliard, 1983, republished with a preface by
Tzvetan Todorov, Paris, Robert Laffont, 2003), see *Le spec-
tateur engagé* [The engaged observer], interviews with
Jean-Louis Missika and Dominique Wolton, Paris, Julliard,
1981, republished Paris, Fallois, 2004.

a path for himself against beloved and esteemed elders. Against the apolitical pacifism of Alain, against the idealist progressivism of Léon Brunschvicg, he measured with more and more anxiety-nourished acuity how much the human lot depends upon the manner in which humans conduct their political life. If the Great War did not suffice to shake the certitudes of numerous French people anxious to resume their prior life, including their prior intellectual life, what was underway on the other side of the Rhine fixed Aron's attention very quickly and set in course the research which was to occupy his life.

In many senses, and as he himself said, Germany was Aron's destiny. Between 1930 and 1933, he went there twice for extended stays, first to Cologne, then to Berlin. He saw Germany, this country that he loved, reject the elementary principles of Euro-

pean life. From his arrival in Cologne, he
experienced the striking sentiment that history was on the march toward the worst.
Nonetheless, it was in Germany that he
found the theoretical tools which allowed
him to intellectually confront the accelera-
tion of events. Max Weber was the hero of
Aron's first maturity. Weber offered to Aron
his relentless curiosity, his capacity to pen-
etrate the most different spiritual universes,
his concern with rigorous causal explana-
tion. He also offered him what was really
lacking in most contemporary French soci-
ologists, the sense of the conflict, of the
drama, and, often, of the tragedy which is
the human adventure. Much later, Aron
would correct what was immoderate or im-
prudent in the Weberian manner of carry-
ing oppositions to their paroxysm, and
sometimes of seeing contradictions, where
a more sober spirit or a more serene heart

would have discerned compatibilities or at least tensions that could be mastered. For example, Aron would later come to doubt that, according to a striking example from Weber, *Les Fleurs du mal* by Baudelaire is beautiful *because* immoral.[3] In any case, in the 1930s, Aron found intellectual equipment in German sociology and in part also the *Stimmung*[4] with which he traversed the dark years.

3. [Note to the French original:] See the introduction of Raymond Aron to the work of Max Weber, *Le savant et le politique* [The scientist and the politician], trad. Julien Freund, Paris, Plon (collection "Recherches en sciences humaines" [Researches in the human sciences]), 1959, p. 52. [Raymond Aron, "Max Weber and Modern Social Science," in *History, Truth, Liberty: Selected Writings of Raymond Aron*, ed. Franciszek Draus (Chicago: University of Chicago Press, 1985), pp. 335–373.]

4. The polysemous term *Stimmung* (mood, temper, tone, tone of voice, mode of articulation) is German in the French original.—Trans.

It's a little before the Second World War that the French and German educations of Aron find their synthetic culmination. In 1938, he defended his dissertation in philosophy: *Introduction to the philosophy of history: An Essay on the limits of historical objectivity.* It's not a question here of giving an account of this detailed study of the "historical condition" of man. Let us only say that in it Aron runs through diverse modes of presence, of experience, and of knowledge of time: from knowledge of self to knowledge of the other, from the diverse intellectual universes in which the individual situates himself to the plurality of perspectives which are offered to him as an actor and as a spectator, as an ordinary man and as an historian. Let us say above all that it's to remain faithful to this plural given of human historicity that Aron vividly criticizes deterministic evolutionism on the one hand, historical relativism on the other, two opposed but equally ruinous strategies to neutralize or to abolish the proper character of the historical condition of man and its specific tragedy, which is precisely that man is neither the lord nor the plaything of time. At the end of this long work, Aron stops and leaves us on a razor's edge. As a result, however "historical" the human condition may be, Aron refuses to derive philosophy from *something other*[5] which would determine it in history. History in his eyes could never become a substitute for philosophy. Following his doctoral thesis, which stands as a final summation of his education, Aron pauses in the posture of a perplexed philosopher, tormented by the human drama: "The possibility of a philosophy of history finally merges with the

5. Italics present in the French original.—Trans.

possibility of a philosophy in defiance of history."[6]

It is the following year that Aron becomes Aron. June 17th, 1939, "between peace and war, in the intermediary regime we live in," Raymond Aron gave a presentation before the French Society of Philosophy: *Democratic States and Totalitarian States*. It is a luminous political analysis, trenchant, sober to the point of asperity, regarding the situation of Europe at the brink of war. Not a word to pander to any party whatsoever, not a syllable to listen to the sound of his own voice. Aron's readings—Pareto, Weber—are put in the service of understanding what makes for

6. [Note to the French original:] *Introduction à la philosophie de l'histoire. Essai sur les limites de l'objectivité historique* (1938) Paris, Gallimard (coll. "Bibliothèque des histoires"), 1967, p. 401. [Aron, *Introduction to the Philosophy of History: An Essay on the Limits of Historical Objectivity*, tr. George J. Irwin (Boston: Beacon Press, 1961), p. 318.]

the respective nature of the totalitarian and democratic regimes, an understanding which is not distorted by the urgencies of action but which nevertheless retains, above all, what matters to the impending action. This renders comprehensible the appeal to *virtù*[7] which provides the tonal note of what Aron many years later will call, with a certain irony, his "moderated Machiavellianism":

> The totalitarian regimes of the 20th century have demonstrated that, if there is a false idea, it is that the administration of things replaces the government of persons. What has appeared in plain clarity is that, when one wants to administer all things, one is obliged, at the same time, to govern all persons.

7. The term *virtù* is Italian in the French original.— Trans.

In the second instance, the necessary condition for democratic survival is to reconstitute a ruling elite, neither cynical nor lax, that would have political courage without falling into Machiavellianism pure and simple. It is necessary, therefore, to have a ruling elite which has confidence in itself and a sense of its own mission.

Finally, and this is the most difficult part, it is necessary to reconstitute in the democratic regimes a minimum of faith or communal will.[8]

8. [Note to the French original:] "Democratic States and Totalitarian States," lecture presented before the French Society of Philosophy on 17 June 1939, published in the *Bulletin de la Société française de philosophie*, n° 2, 1946, in Raymond Aron, *Penser la liberté, penser la démocratie*, éd. et préf. Nicolas Baverez, Paris, Gallimard (coll. "Quarto"), 2005, p[p]. 69–70. [Tr. p. 70.] [Raymond Aron,

The previously unpublished text which we publish here is situated at the other extremity of the career of Raymond Aron. It concerns his last lecture, given on the 4th of April 1978 at the Collège de France. The circumstances were indeed quite different than those which prevailed forty years earlier when Aron intervened before the French Society of Philosophy. At the same time, we can hear this civic unease in Aron's last lecture, which never left him, and which was the core of his life of thought and of action. We can also hear this word which Aron made use of rarely but which he cannot pass over in designating his concern, the word *virtue*:

"Democratic States and Totalitarian States," in Aron, *Thinking Politically: A Liberal in the Age of Ideology*, with an introduction by Daniel J. Mahoney and Brian C. Anderson (New Brunswick, NJ: Transaction Publishers, 1997 [1983]), p. 336.]

But what one no longer knows today in our democracies is where virtue is to be found. Because the theories of democracy and the theories of liberalism always included something like the definition of the virtuous citizen or the manner of life which would conform to the ideal of a free society.[9]

This is what may surprise the reader of today, whether or not he feels sympathy for "Aron the liberal." In fact, our representation of liberalism and even of democracy is dominated by the formal idea of a "procedure," whether it be that of the market or of the guarantee of rights, which would be efficacious by itself and would produce its effects whatever the dispositions of the members of society or of the citizens may

9. [Note to the French original:] See *above*, p. 49.

be. At root, action properly so called, action which can and must be evaluated according to the gradient of the cardinal virtues— more or less courageous, just, prudent, etc.—, no longer has much of a place among us, since the sole virtue demanded of us is the application of rules which, necessarily, will satisfy our interests and guarantee our rights. For a long time one continued to oppose the consumer to the citizen, or even the producer to the citizen. In speaking so willfully of the "citizen consumer" or of the "civic enterprise," we betray the extent to which we have lost the sense of civic life. The life and reflection of Aron unfolded in a wholly other climate. Perhaps the anxiety which has seized the European democracies for the past several years does not derive solely from the economic and financial crisis, but from the loss of the substance of civic life which requires our full attention. Aron's unease may contribute to our education.

Our political anxiety derives in good measure from our intellectual perplexity, and this, in turn, results largely from the confusion which surrounds the notion of "liberalism." For a long time, Raymond Aron was, along with Bertrand de Jouvenel, the principal representative of French liberalism. At the same time, one may assert that liberalism as such, liberalism as a doctrine and even as a program, only rarely furnished the theme of his reflections. It informed his dispositions, gave him elements of orientation, but one may not characterize Aron's approach as the intention to apply a liberal doctrine. It would be more just to say that he was forced to study the political as such, according to the diversity of its forms and regimes, it being understood that in his eyes the experience of modern centuries tended to establish that a liberal *politics* offered the best chance for rationality, and more broadly furnished the frame of a human life worthy of living. For him, it seems to me, liberalism may be an attribute but never a substance. Consequently this larger, which is to say, political, understanding of liberalism has been obscured under the combined influence of the enemies of liberalism and of its systematic theorists—under the combined influence of Carl Schmitt and of Friedrich Hayek. The first famously decreed that "there is not a liberal politics *sui generis*, there is only a liberal *critique* of the political."[10] As for the second, he developed an

---

10. [Note to the French original:] See Carl Schmitt, *La notion de politique* [*The Concept of the Political*], tr. Marie-Louise Steinhauser, preface by Julien Freund (Paris: Calmann-Lévy (coll. "Liberté de l'esprit"), 1972), p. 117.

impressive theory of what he called the "spontaneous order," that order which results from human actions but not from human designs. Order here appears as a system of action of which the market furnishes the model, which does not, at root, have anything properly political about it, and which even tends to render the political superfluous, since it has nothing better to do than to respectfully preserve this system of action.[11] In an otherwise rather admiring essay[12] on Hayek's most synthetic work, *The Constitution*

11. [Note to the French original:] See the recent book by Edwige Kacenelenbogen, *Le nouvel idéal politique* [*The New Political Ideal*], with a foreword by Pierre Manent (Paris: Éditions de l'EHESS (coll. "En temps et lieux"), 2013).

12. [Note to the French original:] "La définition libérale de la liberté" (1961), in *Les sociétés modernes*, éd. et intr. Serge Paugam, Paris, PUF (coll. "Quadrige"), 2006, p[p]. 627–646. [See Aron, "The Liberal Definition of Liberty, Concerning F. A. Hayek's *The Constitution of Liberty*,"

of Liberty,[13] Aron discloses most clearly the property of his political liberalism, or, rather, of his liberal politics. It is in contrast with Hayek's liberalism that the political thought of Aron comes most clearly to light.

Aron's intellectual style and the spirit of his liberal politics appear with a perfect clarity in the following lines:

The goal of a free society ought to be to limit to the greatest extent possible the government of men by men and to constrain the government of men by laws. Such is, no doubt about it, the first imperative of liberalism as Hayek conceives it. It so happens that, personally, I share

---

in *In Defense of Political Reason*, ed. Daniel Mahoney (Lanham, MD: Rowman and Littlefield, 1994), pp. 73–91.]

13. The title of Hayek's work is in English in the French original.—Trans.

this ideal. The reservations which I shall formulate do not, therefore, have their origin in a different hierarchy of values but in the consideration of several facts.[14]

Among these "several facts," there is the plurality of "human collectivities," and, therefore, the necessity of directing their relations, "direction of external politics [which] remains the work of men and not of laws." For, "Hayek, like most liberals, does not treat of foreign politics. He restricts himself, in passing, to noting that, provisionally, the world State appears to

14. [Note to the French original:] Ibid., p[p]. [637–] 638. [*Les sociétés modernes*, ed. Serge Paugam (Paris: PUF, 2006), pp. 627–646.] [See Raymond Aron, "The Liberal Definition of Liberty, Concerning F. A. Hayek's *The Constitution of Liberty*," in Aron, *In Defense of Political Reason*, ed. Daniel Mahoney (Lanham, MD: Rowman and Littlefield, 1994), pp. 82–83.]

him to be dangerous for individual liberty and that it would be better, in these circumstances, to accommodate oneself to the plurality of States and their possible wars."[15] We may note in passing that this indifference of the doctrinaire liberals to the questions of external politics and, more generally, to the de facto plurality of political bodies is widely shared today, the reigning postulate in Europe being that, under the inherited divisions and borders of the past, human unity is irresistibly on its way to being realized. If "ultra-liberalism" is denounced by many, its ultimate horizon is shared by most: humanity tends to organize itself spontaneously according to a

15. [Note to the French original:] Ibid. [*Les sociétés modernes*, ed. Serge Paugam (Paris: PUF, 2006), p. 638.] [Aron, *In Defense of Political Reason*, ed. Daniel Mahoney (Lanham, MD: Rowman and Littlefield, 1994), p. 83.]

worldwide system of action, the harmony of which is only menaced by the obstinacy of old nations and ancient religions wanting, incomprehensibly, to preserve themselves in being. Aron dedicated perhaps a good third of his immense commentary on contemporary politics to strategic questions and international politics. If, as an attentive reader of Auguste Comte, Aron measured the power of the *process* which conduced toward the dynamic unification of humanity in a history which had become universal, he kept his eyes open for the endlessly renewed possibilities of the inseparable *drama* of the coexistence between political bodies and heterogeneous religious groups.[16]

16. [Note to the French original:] "What separates men from one another most is what each holds sacred. A pagan or Jew who will not convert is offering a challenge

Perhaps the blindness or indifference of Hayek in the face of certain major facts of our political condition derives ultimately from a paralogism, one quite simple and widespread. Hayek takes as given what is in question; he takes as his point of departure what, in the best of cases, may only be a destination. More precisely, with the aim of

to a Christian. Is someone who is ignorant of the God of the religions of salvation our neighbor or a stranger with whom we can have nothing in common? But it is with him that we shall have to build a spiritual community, which is the superstructure or foundation of the physical community, which tends to be created by the unity of science, technology, and economics, a unity imposed by the historic destiny of a mankind more conscious of its differences than of its solidarity." In "L'aube de l'histoire universelle" ["The dawn of universal history"] (1960), *Penser la liberté, penser la démocratie* [*Thinking liberty, thinking democracy*], op. cit., p[p]. 1806–1807. [Raymond Aron, "The Dawn of Universal History," in Aron, *The Dawn of Universal History*, ed. Yair Reiner, tr. Barbara Bray (New York: Basic Books, 2002), pp. 484–485.]

seeing the ascendance of the spontaneous order of the free actions of individual agents, as a presupposition he grants himself such agents, he presupposes them capable of valuing their rights and their talents while respecting common rules. But such agents are not born in the cabbage patch! Aron writes a little later on:

> The ideal of a society in which each may choose his gods or his values cannot spread before individuals have been educated to collective life. The philosophy of Hayek takes for granted, by definition, the results that the philosophers of the past considered the primary objects of political action. To allow to each a private sphere of decision and of choice, it is necessary that all or most already want to live together and recognize the same system of ideas as true, the same formula

of legitimacy as valid. Before society can be liberal, it is necessary that it should exist.[17]

This conviction of Aron that political goods are difficult things to produce and that they have, at the very least, to be *wanted*, founds a quite marked scepticism with respect to a European citizenship which others pretend is easy to obtain because at root it should already exist. In an article from 1974 which has lost none of its relevance, and which finds today a relevance even more acute, Aron raises the argument so often reprised according to which "Europeans become Europeans without be-

17. [Note to the French original:] "La définition libérale de la liberté" ["The liberal definition of liberty"], art. cit., p. 642. [Aron, *In Defense of Political Reason*, ed. Daniel Mahoney (Lanham, MD: Rowman and Littlefield, 1994), p. 86.]

coming conscious of the fact" because "they live the same life together wholly while imagining that they live the narrow life of the past."[18] He shows little faith in this kind of civic education which formed European citizens by capillarity. He highlights the weakness of an opinion favourable to Europe but following a passive mode which in no way promises any political effect, an opinion elsewhere frustrated or discouraged by the indecipherability of the European political landscape. More radically, in foreseeing that one will undoubtedly reproach him with "the classicism, if not the anachronism of [his] analysis," he

18. [Note to the French original:] "Une citoyenneté multinationale est-elle possible?" ["Is a multinational citizenship possible?"], in *Les sociétés modernes* [*Modern Societies*], op cit., p. 791. [Raymond Aron, "Is Multinational Citizenship Possible?" *Social Research* 41:4 (Winter, 1974), pp. 638–656, at p. 649.]

highlights that which is specific, irreducible, difficult, and urgent in citizenship, which is in no way included in shared humanity:

> History has therefore confirmed the distinction between the rights of man and those of the citizen. The rights which the *Declaration* [*of the Rights of Man and Citizen*] enumerated pertain, some to men as such, others to citizens, therefore, to members of a political collectivity. By this term, I mean a collectivity capable, within the interior of a certain territory, of imposing respect for the rights recognized to individuals and reciprocally of the duties which the collectivity imposes.
>
> In fact, whoever has known the experience of the loss of his political collectivity has felt the existential anguish (however temporary) of solitude; what

is it that remains to the individual, in the periods of crisis, of his human rights, when he no longer belongs to any political collectivity?[19]

Aron's half-ironic remark on this objection which he foresees inspires us and may lend us support to extend his reflections: Aron is a liberal *classical* thinker rather than a classical *liberal* thinker. Aron—a classical thinker? Is he not, rather, very much a *modern*, always encouraging the modernization of the economy, of the administration, of education, and, in general, encouraging the modernization of the French way of life, without the least trace of nostalgia for "the world we have lost," offering commentary

19. [Note to the French original:] Ibid., p. 794. [Tr. Ibid., pp. 793–794.] [Raymond Aron, "Is Multinational Citizenship Possible?" *Social Research* 41:4 (Winter, 1974), pp. 638–656, at p. 652.]

on the INSEE[20] index of the day, rather than on the dialogues of Plato? All this is true, but precisely, if he does not feel nostalgia for the Greek city nor indeed for the "ages of faith," neither does he nourish intemperate hopes in progress or in "modernity," and this mastery of the affects, this sobriety in approaching human affairs, and especially in approaching political things, which are always susceptible of "bearing" us away, is what merits the qualifier of classical. This does not here refer back to works or epochs particularly worthy of admiration, but more essentially to what I shall call a virile acceptance of the limits within which human life operates and at the center of

20. INSEE is the acronym for the Institut National de la Statistique et des Études Économiques, the National Institute of Statistics and Economic Studies, which studies and measures, among other things, economic growth in France.—Trans.

which human life may find the full accomplishment of its capabilities. It's within these limits that liberalism and, in general, modern inventions or instruments can make a claim for and merit our approbation or our adhesion, for the visible improvements which they bring to the human lot.

This classicism illustrates itself particularly in the manner in which Aron conducted his political and sociological inquiries, and of which one finds another example in the lecture at the Collège de France which we publish here. Aron does not proceed in the manner of the theoreticians of liberalism who, like John Locke, depart from a solitary individual discovering his rights at the same time as his needs in the state of nature, and conceptually elaborate the political instrument—the sovereign and representative State—capable of guaranteeing those rights and of favoring the satisfaction

of those needs. It is sometimes said that
Aron, as a philosopher, belonged to the
Kantian school broadly understood, and he
himself did not discourage this suggestion.
The most that may be said in this regard is
that when he takes it upon himself, and this
is quite rare, to designate what his perspective or his ultimate horizon would be, he
freely mentions as a "regulating idea," a sort
of "kingdom of ends" of humanity in which
each man would be for the other an end
and not only a means. But precisely this
idea of reason, however legitimate and perhaps encouraging it may be, in no way helps
to determine the analysis and the choices of
political understanding, and it's on this
plane of political understanding that Aron
is always essentially situated. In truth, without the presupposition of the state of nature,
of a best regime, or of an idea of reason,
Aron accepts, to employ the language of

cards, the "hand" which history dealt him, and he installs his post of observation in the midst of the effective and present conditions of political life. If one must give him a referent in the history of philosophy, then it is no one other than Aristotle, the father and master of political science, who, scrupulously analyzing the real, also discerns within it that which is possible, including the "best possible."

For Aron as for Aristotle, it is a matter of beginning from what is. This seems to be the easiest thing in the world, does it not? However, *we* begin by doing just the opposite: we judge, which is to say, most often, sovereignly condemn the existing regime, the society of which we are members, in the name of a past glory, or of the regime to come, or we choose amongst those characteristics with which we agree, relegating the connected characteristic to the hell of "ideology." And each person, furnished with a scalpel, strictly separates the good liberty from the bad, the good equality from the bad, etc. It is true that it is up to us to judge, but only after having listened to the parties involved. Let us not begin by deciding that the world is wrong. The world is obscure, it is true, but our clear ideas are perhaps too clear. Beginning from what is therefore consists in taking seriously the ruling opinions, not for adhering to them docilely but to seek in them those elements of orientation without which we will never do anything other than oppose the confusion of the world with the false clarity of ideas chosen by our passions. And this is what Aron did with rigor and scruple which have often received wholly other names.[21] They have been ranged under the etiquette

---

21. Implicitly, from Aron's detractors.—Trans.

of "realism," of "eclecticism," of "conserva-
tism," the approach of a spirit supposed to be
too timid to elevate itself toward the ideal or
determine the true liberty or equality. In
fact, to the indignation or to the regrets not
only of the left but of a great part of the right,
liberal or not, Aron *accepted* the great characteristics of modern society and of the
modern regime. Not only capitalism but
State provision, not only the formal liberties,
which he judged to be amongst the most
real, but social rights which, as one will read
below, he counted amongst the liberties.
This was bound to be displeasing to all parties. It was not that Aron was incapable of
choosing, it was that he measured the ambi-
guity, the polyvalence of the founding notions of modern politics, and, above all, of
liberty and equality.

To begin from what is, for Aron as for
Aristotle, is to begin from "opinions" which

have authority in the society considered. To begin from the "opinions," here, from liberty and from equality, is not to begin from the "ideas" such as these are elaborated by philosophy or science, but such as they orient human evaluations and actions. For example, at the beginning of the lecture which you are about to read,[22] Aron considers article 4 of the *Declaration of the Rights of Man and Citizen* of 1789, with the famous clause: "Liberty consists in the ability to do whatever does not harm another." He offers this stunning and, at first glance, disappointing commentary: "This formula is, at once, in one sense evident and in another sense almost denuded of meaning." One is frustrated by this commentary up until one ascertains that it is perfectly founded. Evident and at the

22. Manent's text here was originally printed as an introduction to the transcript of the Aron lecture.—Trans.

same time almost denuded of sense, there's the rub. And it is indeed the proof that this formula is not a philosophic thesis, as philosophic theses are, in general, neither evident nor denuded of sense! Liberty is the object of a new determination, a new meaning added to the ancient meanings without abolishing them, the liberty of the individual is added to those of the citizen and of the moral man, and this new determination introduces a novel indeterminacy in the social, moral, and political apparatus. What is the result of all this? Only the analysis and above all the most impartial description possible, such as what Aron attempts in this lecture, is in a position to specify it.

The mention of Aristotle here is not decorative. It is used to refer to a political and social science which does not reject but reclaims judgments of value. Judgments which only intervene after the parties have been heard, as I already said, judgments borne with sobriety and in a spirit of impartiality, as I also already said, but in the end judgments of value without which neither life nor science are possible. If Weber, as we have seen, was the declared hero of Aron's first maturity, Aristotle silently accompanied his social and political inquiry once it had effectively begun. Weber gave a powerful encouragement to Aron's program of life and science, but at the point of the realization of the program, it was conducted more according to the spirit of Aristotle than of Weber.

Moreover, Aron's abandonment of what is immoderate in Weber's irrationalism has not remained implicit. As I have already alluded, in his introduction to *Le savant et le politique*, Aron amiably but firmly dismisses the "bellicose and pathetic" vision of Max Weber. It will suffice to cite the following:

Whatever his choice may be, [the philosopher] does not take notice of the "war of the gods." If the philosopher adheres to utopia, he conserves the hope of reconciliation. If he is wise, therefore, resigned to the unwisdom of others, why would he see an inexpiable conflict between himself and those who are insensate, between those who meditate and those who fight? The hero neither ignores nor contemns the saint: he contemns the one who turns the other cheek through cowardice, not the one who turns the other cheek through a superior courage.

Why is Max Weber assured at this point that the conflicts of Olympus are inexpiable? Both because the conflicts were within him and because these conflicts are the privileged object of sociological study. The rationalist recognized the battle between faith and unbelief, he admitted that neither the one nor the other was scientifically demonstrable. All the while subscribing to the truth of unbelief, the rationalist does not derive the conclusion of the war of the gods, but of the progressive diffusion of the Enlightenment or even of the persistence of illusions. In the eyes of the believer, on the contrary, it is faith which fixes the sense of scepticism. The formula of the "war of the gods" is the transposition of an indisputable fact—men create for themselves incompatible representations of the world—into a philosophy which no one either sees or reflects upon because it is contradictory.[23]

23. [Note to the French original:] See Max Weber, *Le savant et le politique*, introduction, op. cit., pp. 54–55. [Raymond Aron, "Max Weber and Modern Social Science," in

The lecture which we shall read is not situated upon these peaks. It is no less worthy of interest for its inquiry into a common or shared truth in societies—ours—which appear more indifferent to truth, or, if one prefers, societies that seem to have made an unreserved choice for liberty to the detriment of truth, or even to the detriment of the search for truth. Aron invokes no truth to oppose to the anarchy of desires consecrated in their rights, he does not even rebuff contemporary hedonism for its demeanor against any limit which might restrain it, but he interrogates the "moral crisis of liberal democracies." The unease which works upon liberal democracies, and which may translate into the most unreasonable conduct, is

---

History, Truth, Liberty: Selected Writings of Raymond Aron, ed. Franciszek Draus (Chicago: University of Chicago Press, 1985), pp. 335–373.]

a sign that they may not resign themselves to the absence if not of a common truth, at least of a common good largely shared. But being obstinate in their dogmatic scepticism, they deprive liberty of the elements of orientation without which it is condemned to wither more or less rapidly. One may well receive these observations coming from such a benevolent witness.

The lecture was thus delivered in April 1978. In what measure does the proposed description hold for contemporary liberal democracies? What we have said suggests that in many ways Aron speaks of us. Where he is concerned with liberty detached from any criterion, with very generally recognized democratic legitimacy, with the absence of an accepted notion of virtue or of the common good, we recognize ourselves. What, in Aron's description, draws us back to a time which has disappeared is the evocation of the "anarchic" rejection of society as much, of its institutions and works, it's the postulation amongst certain persons of another society or of a wholly other society, of another "community." Partially, this tendency has since been paradoxically socialized, integrated into the present society, because this society has largely done away with authoritarian institutions which made citizens feel their subordination to the social whole. It suffices to mention the suppression of military service. At the same time, this society thus "distended" is more and more uneasy about losing those institutions which guaranteed its cohesion. At the same time that the libertarian disposition has installed itself, to the point of taking its ease, the demand for security has made itself felt more and more, and expresses itself in phenomena as different as the asphyxiating proliferation of public health regulations,

or the obsession with pollution, or the dis-
ciplining of public speech under the regime
said to be "politically correct," to say nothing of the centrality of the Ministry of the
Interior in the governments of the Republic
over the past decade. More than ever "liberty consists in being able to do whatever
does not harm another," and in consequence whatever is possible to do, including whatever is possible to say, is more and
more circumscribed in proportion that the
feeling of what "harms" or may harm ex-
pands and is vibrant. "Everything afflicts
me, and harms me, and conspires to harm
me," the contemporary citizen seems to say.
A discouraging perception is at the basis of
this civic atonality which Aron diagnosed
on the eve of the second oil crisis.

One will note that, however troubled he
may have been by certain developments,
Aron accuses no one. It happens that in a

political body, and this is how he defines it, the citizens, as they share in the common good, together partake in the weaknesses and, as one likes to say today, in the "pathologies" of the city. Perhaps they partake unequally, but all partake. The impartiality of the benevolent and participant observer is the beginning of recovery. The glance of the wise encourages the virtue of the citizen.[24]

24. [Note to the French original:] I thank Giulio De Ligio, a researcher associated with the Raymond Aron Center for Political and Social Research, for the help which he has given me in preparing this text.